Cherise the niece

Cherise the niece

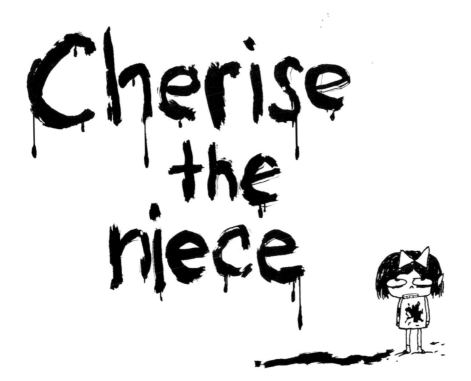

J. K. Benton

A PLUME BOOK

PLUME
Published by the Penguin Group
Penguin Group (USA) Inc., 375 Hudson Street, New York, New York 10014, U.S.A. • Penguin Group (Canada), 90 Eglinton Avenue East, Suite 700, Toronto, Ontario, Canada M4P 2Y3 (a division of Pearson Penguin Canada Inc.) • Penguin Books Ltd., 80 Strand, London WC2R ORL, England • Penguin Ireland, 25 St. Stephen's Green, Dublin 2, Ireland (a division of Penguin Books Ltd.) • Penguin Group (Australia), 250 Camberwell Road, Camberwell, Victoria 3124, Australia (a division of Pearson Australia Group Pty. Ltd.) • Penguin Books India Pvt. Ltd., 11 Community Centre, Panchsheel Park, New Delhi – 110 017, India • Penguin Group (NZ), 67 Apollo Drive, Rosedale, North Shore 0632, New Zealand (a division of Pearson New Zealand Ltd.) • Penguin Books (South Africa) (Pty.) Ltd., 24 Sturdee Avenue, Rosebank, Johannesburg 2196, South Africa

Penguin Books Ltd., Registered Offices: 80 Strand, London WC2R ORL, England

First published by Plume, a member of Penguin Group (USA) Inc.

First Printing, June 2008
10 9 8 7 6 5 4 3 2 1

Copyright © Jim Benton, 2008

 REGISTERED TRADEMARK—MARCA REGISTRADA

CIP data is available.
ISBN 978-0-452-228948-2

Printed in Mexico

Set in Cleanhouse
Designed by Daniel Lagin

BOOKS ARE AVAILABLE AT QUANTITY DISCOUNTS WHEN USED TO PROMOTE PRODUCTS OR SERVICES. FOR INFORMATION PLEASE WRITE TO PREMIUM MARKETING DIVISION, PENGUIN GROUP (USA) INC., 375 HUDSON STREET, NEW YORK, NEW YORK 10014.

No Aunts or cats were harmed in the writing of this book.
Under no circumstances should people harm other people
or cats even if they are Aunts. And besides, Cherise is
a fictitious character. Although, if I was an Aunt, I'd
probably check under my bed tonight just in case we're
wrong about that part.

To our nieces, whom we love in spite of our suspicions.

Cherise the niece

She was orphaned quite young.
In a mysterious way,
Her parents just up and
Vanished one day.

But Cherise muddled through
This most odd circumstance
Through the generous, loving
Support of her Aunts.

Take
Her

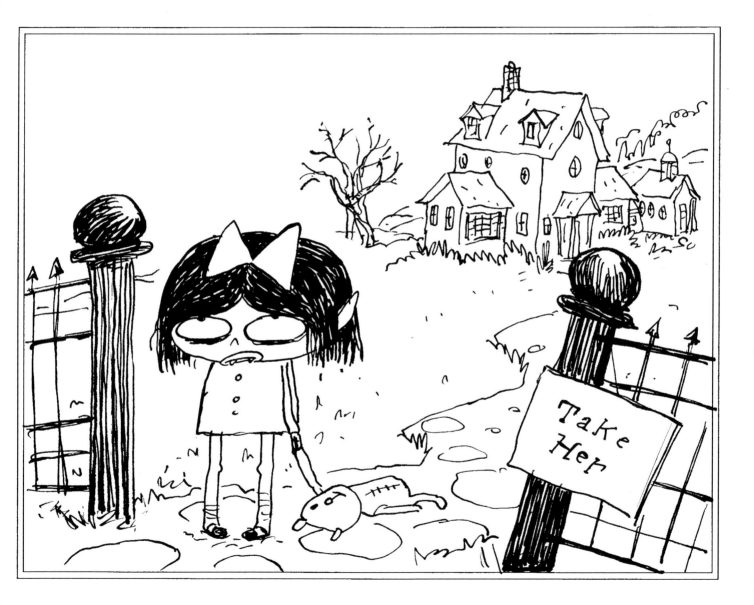

She stayed for a while,
With her dear old Aunt Bea,
'Til one day when bug spray
Wound up in her tea.

She was sent way up North
To stay with Aunt Flo,
Who disappeared strangely
Right after a snow.

She stayed with an Aunt
And her sweet little dog,
Who Cherise said she saw
Roll her up like a log.

She was then taken in
By Aunt Betty Lou,
Who liked to bake things
And Cherise liked it, too.

KITT

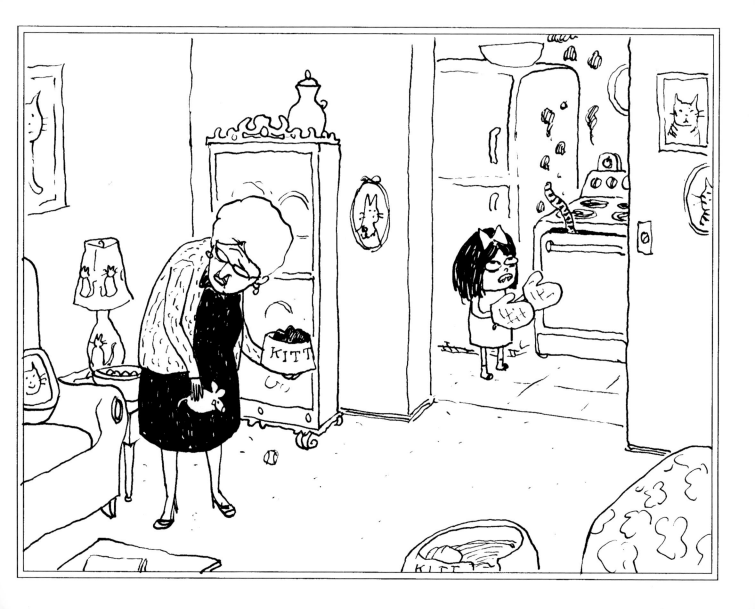

But she dropped a few hints
About wanting to stay
With her Aunt by the sea,
Who dropped in the next day.

CAUTION

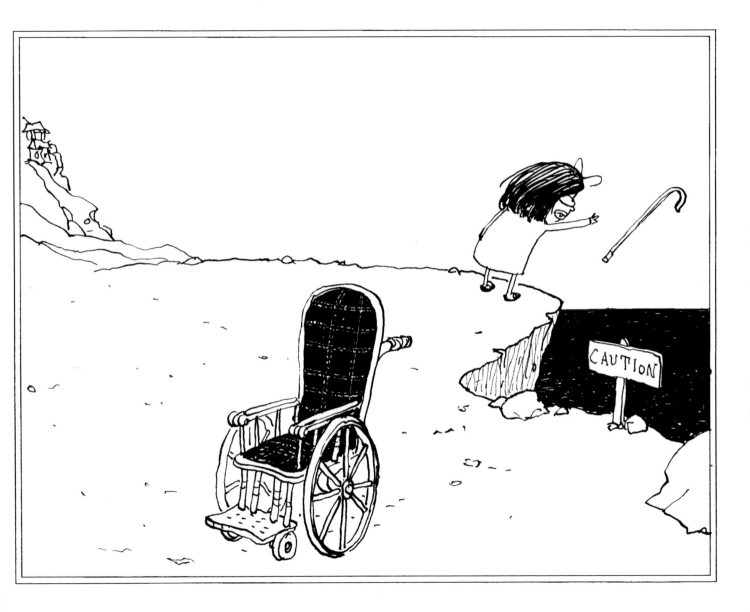

Auntie Rose loved her garden
Though Cherise despised it.
But together, one Wednesday
They both fertilized it.

On a picnic one day,
Aunt May drowned in the river,
But what made it much worse
Was Cherise got a sliver.

Aunt Annie and Fanny
Gave Cherise an aquarium.
Now the family's discussing
Just where they should bury 'em.

That winter she went
To stay with Aunt Summer.
The spring was quite nice,
But her fall was a bummer.

Aunt Meg painted her
In the costume of Cupid,
But Cherise made the point
That she thought it was stupid.

While decking the halls
With boughs of holly,
The star must have slipped
And decked her Aunt Molly.

LIGHTS
STAR

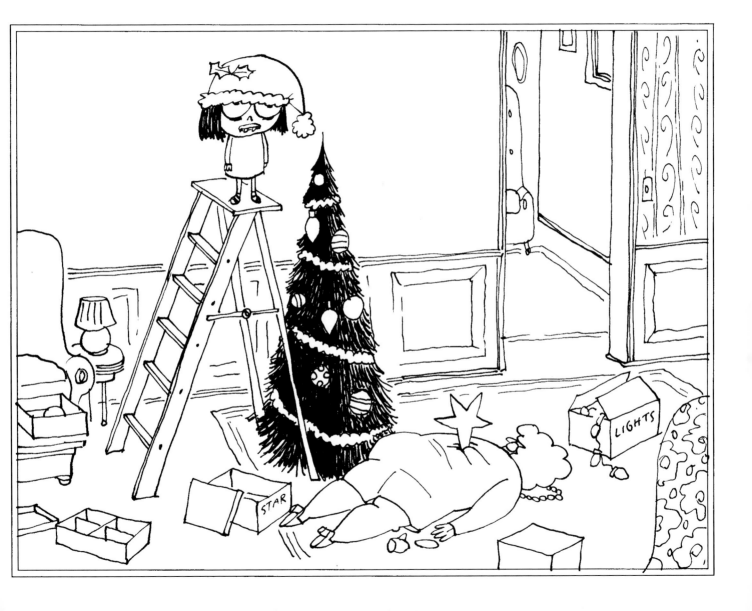

For Cherise, it was over—
That had been her last chance
At a warm, loving family.
She was fresh out of Aunts.

They told her the orphanage
Was where she must go.
But Cherise softly uttered:

To
Orphanage

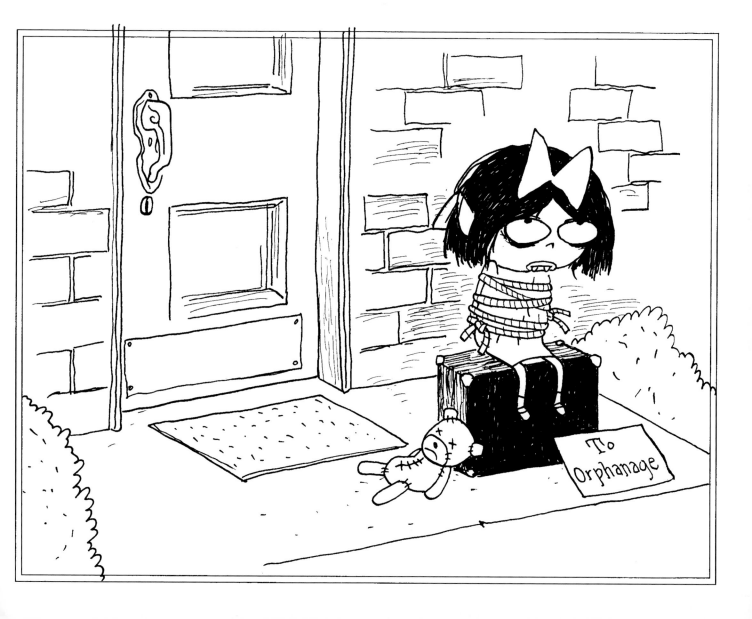

I have Uncles, you know.

ADDRESS BOOK

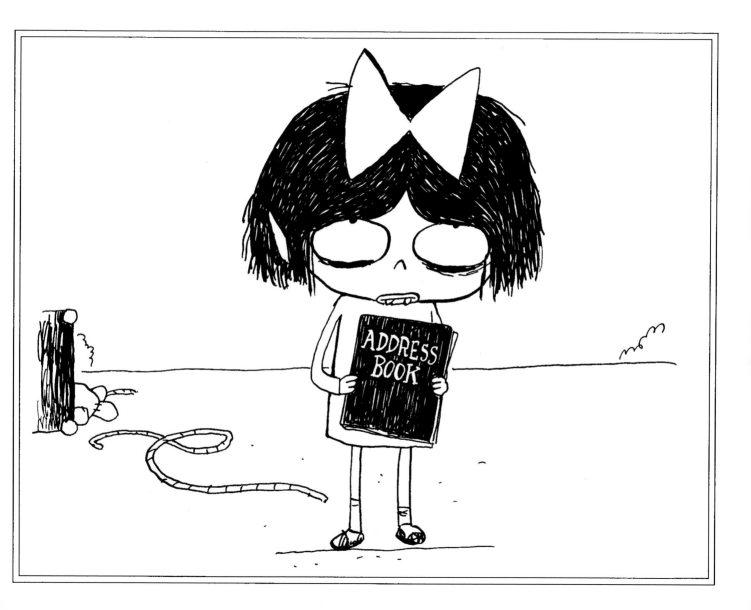

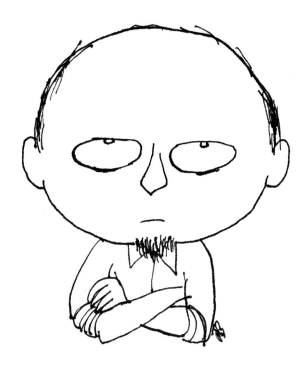

Jim Benton is a writer and artist who might draw a happy bunny one moment, and then turn around and write poems about a scary little niece the next. It's probably best to not ask why.

Visit www.cherisetheniece.com